Table of contents

Introduction

First of all I would like to say thank you for purchasing this book. Now I will give you a short overview of this book. Dump dinners have created so much comfort in my life and now I do not waste my extra time in kitchen. Dump dinners recipes allow me to serve my extra time with my family. In dump recipes you have no need to serve hours in kitchen, in fact just prepare baking dish containing all ingredients and then bake it in oven. The taste of these recipes is unmatchable and quality is awesome. Dump dinners are good in taste but at the same time good for health.

In this book I have included real dump dinner's recipes and not just slow cooker recipes. All recipes included in this book will be prepared in oven.

Always keep in mind that dump dinners which you bake in oven have far better taste then slow cooker recipes.

I have included 40 fine Dump dinners' recipes in this book and I hope you will enjoy this book a lot. Most of recipe included in this book are unseen and unique. This book also contains desserts recipes. So let,s dive into book and start enjoying amazing dump dinner recipes.

Hobo Dump Dinner

What ingredients you will need:

salt to taste

ground black pepper to taste

garlic salt to taste

1 pound ground beef

5 potatoes, peeled and cut into steak fries

4 large carrots, peeled and sliced lengthwise

1 onion, peeled and sliced into rings

Directions:

1) First of all preheat oven to 400 degrees F. Now take a 9x13 inch baking dish which should be lined with aluminum foil.

2) Make small patties from ground beef and put them in baking dish.

3) Now add vegetables on beef patties and make layers of vegetables.

4) Finally sprinkle garlic salt, pepper and salt according to your taste.

5) After covering and sealing it with aluminum foil place baking dish in preheated oven for baking.

6) Now bake it in oven for 1 hour.

7) Recipe is ready to serve. Serve and enjoy. You will get 4 servings in total.

Nutritional facts per serving:

Serving size: 350g

Calories: 470kcal

Carbohydrates: 43g

Protein: 27g

Fat: 11g

Fiber: 9g

===================

Dumpy Parmesan Chicken

What ingredients you will need:

1/4 pound butter, melted

2 tablespoons chopped fresh parsley

1 cup dried bread crumbs

1 clove crushed garlic

1/3 cup grated Parmesan cheese

1 teaspoon salt

1/8 teaspoon ground black pepper

1 (4 pound) chicken, cut into pieces

Directions:

1)   First of all preheat oven to 350 degrees F. Take a mixing bowl and mix crushed garlic and melted butter in it.

2)   Now in another bowl mix salt, pepper, cheese, parsley and bread crumbs and make a crumbs mixture.

3)   After dipping chicken pieces with garlic butter mixture coat them with crumbs mixture. Take a 9x13 inch baking dish and make it greasy.

4)   Put coated chicken pieces in greasy baking dish. Pour remaining mixture of garlic butter mixture on top of chicken.

5)   Place baking dish in oven for baking process. Bake it in oven for 60 to 80 minutes and enjoy tasty parmesan chicken.

6)   Serve and enjoy. You will get 6 servings in total.

Nutritional facts per serving:

Serving size: 250g

Calories: 410kcal

Carbohydrates: 14g

Protein: 57g

Fat: 41g

Fiber: 1g

========================

Dumped Fish Dinner

What ingredients you will need:

4 cloves garlic, minced

1 zucchini, thickly sliced

4 tablespoons olive oil, divided

2 baking potatoes, cut into 1/2 inch slices

2 stalks celery, cut into thin 3 inch long slices

1 pound white fish fillets

1 tomato, seeded and chopped

2 sprigs fresh parsley or fennel, for garnish

salt and pepper to taste

1/2 cup water

1/2 red bell pepper, chopped

1 leek, bulb only, chopped

Directions:

1)   First of all preheat oven to 425 degrees F. Take a 2 quart baking dish and make it greasy.

2)   In a mixing bowl add potatoes and then pour olive oil on top of it. Sprinkle salt and pepper on it and then place potatoes in baking dish along with 1/4 cup water.

3)   Bake potatoes in oven after covering for 15 minutes.

4)   In another bowl mix celery, leek, zucchini and bell peppers. Now add garlic, salt, pepper and olive oil in it and mix all ingredients very well.

5)   Place these vegetables on baked potatoes along with 1/4 cup water and bake again after covering for 10 to 15 minutes.

6)   Finally place fish pieces in shape of cubes on top of vegetables. Place baking dish oven and bake t for 15 minutes or until fish gets

desired tenderness.

7)   Dumped Fish Dinner is ready to serve. Serve and enjoy. You will get 4 servings in total.

Nutritional facts per serving:

Serving size: 270g

Calories: 450kcal

Carbohydrates: 28g

Protein: 21g

Fat: 30g

Fiber: 5g

= = = = = = = = = = = = = = = = = = = =

Dump Barbecue Chicken

What ingredients you will need:

1 cup ketchup

3 tablespoons butter

2 tablespoons Worcestershire sauce

1 tablespoon onion powder

10 chicken wings

5 tablespoons brown sugar

1/2 cup water

2 tablespoons prepared mustard

Directions:

1)   First of all preheat oven to 425 degrees F. Take a sauce pan and melt butter in it. Add Worcestershire sauce, mustard onion powder and

sugar in saucepan.

2)   After diluting ketchup with water add it to saucepan and simmer this mixture for 15 to 20 minutes.

3)   Take a 9x13 inch size baking dish and add chicken wings in it. Pour prepared mixture on top of chicken and place this baking dish in oven for baking process.

4)   Bake it in oven for 45 minutes.

5)   Dump Barbecue Chicken is ready to serve. Serve and enjoy.

6)   This original recipe will give you 6 servings in total.

Nutritional facts per serving:

Serving size: 250g

Calories: 380kcal

Carbohydrates: 27g

Protein: 20g

Fat: 23g

Fiber: 1g

= = = = = = = = = = = = = = = = = = = =

Veggie Chicken

What ingredients you will need:

3 carrots, coarsely chopped

1 green bell pepper, sliced

2 onions, peeled and cut into chunks

2 tomatoes, dice

6 chicken thighs

1 tablespoon vegetable oil

1 teaspoon garlic powder

1 teaspoon ground allspice

1 teaspoon dried parsley

1 teaspoon paprika

salt and pepper to taste

4 potatoes, peeled and quartered

2 tablespoons olive oil

Directions:

1)   First of all preheat oven to 325 degrees F. Take a 9x13 inch size baking dish and make it greasy with the help of 1 tablespoon of vegetable oil.

2) Sprinkle salt, pepper, allspice, parsley, paprika and garlic powder on chicken pieces and then put them in the baking dish.

3)   Now add all vegetables on chicken and pour 2 tablespoons of olive oil on top of it.

4) Now place this baking dish in oven after covering with aluminum foil for baking process. Bake it in pre heated oven for 60 minutes.

5)   Make sure that chicken should not be pinkish in color and potatoes should be tender.

6)   Veggie Chicken is ready to serve.

7)   Serve and enjoy. This original recipe will give you 6 servings in total.

Serving size: 250g

Calories: 410kcal

Carbohydrates: 22g

Protein: 40g

Fat: 21g

Fiber: 11g

=====================

Dumped Beef Ribs

What ingredients you will need:

2 tablespoons all-purpose flour

2 pounds beef short ribs

1/3 cup soy sauce

1/4 cup brown sugar

1/2 cup olive oil

4 cloves garlic, minced

1 pinch curry powder

Directions:

1)   Take a large pot and fill it with water. Add ribs in it and boil for 20 minutes.

2)   Preheat oven to 425 degrees F.

3)   Take a mixing bowl and mix olive oil, flour, curry powder, soy sauce, brown sugar and garlic in it and make a sauce.

4)   Now after draining ribs coat them with prepared mixture.

5)   Place these ribs in a baking dish.

6)   Put baking dish in the pre heated oven and bake it for 30 minutes.

7)   If there is any remaining sauce then pour it on ribs.

8)   Dumped Beef Ribs are ready to serve. Serve and enjoy.

9)   This original recipe will give you 3 servings in total.

Nutritional facts per serving:

Serving size: 550g

Calories: 910kcal

Carbohydrates: 21g

Protein: 47g

Fat: 91g

Fiber: 11g

= = = = = = = = = = = = = = = = = = = =

Baked Catfish

What ingredients you will need:

1/2 teaspoon ground black pepper

1 teaspoon dried thyme

1 1/2 pounds catfish fillets

1/2 cup yellow cornmeal

1 teaspoon paprika

1/2 teaspoon onion powder

1/2 teaspoon garlic powder

1 teaspoon salt

1/2 teaspoon celery seed

1/2 cup skim milk

cooking spray

Directions:

1)   First of all preheat oven to 325 degrees F. Now take a baking dish which should be lined with aluminum foil. Make it greasy with the help of cooking spray.

2)   In a mixing bowl mix all other ingredients except catfish and make a mixture.

3)   Coat catfish fillets with prepared mixture and put them in greasy baking sheet.

4)   Now place baking dish in the oven for baking process. Bake it in oven for 15 to 20 minutes.

5)   Baked Catfish is ready to serve. Serve and enjoy.

6)   This original recipe will give you 6 servings in total.

Nutritional facts per serving:

Serving size: 150g

Calories: 220kcal

Carbohydrates: 11g

Protein: 20g

Fat: 9g

Fiber: 1g

=====================

Oven Brown Rice with Carrots and Mushrooms

What ingredients you will need:

1 (14 ounce) can beef broth

cooking spray

1 cup uncooked brown rice

1/2 cup milk

1 cup finely diced carrots

1 (4 ounce) can sliced mushrooms, drained

1/2 cup condensed cream of chicken soup

1/4 cup butter

Directions:

1)   First of all preheat oven to 350 degrees F. Take a casserole dish and make it greasy with the help of cooking spray.

2)   Take a large size mixing bowl and add all ingredients in it. Now mix all ingredients very well and make a mixture.

3)   Pour prepared mixture in greasy casserole dish and place it in the oven.

4)   Bake it in oven for 60 minutes or until rice are tender.

5)   Oven Brown Rice with Carrots and Mushrooms is ready to serve. Serve and enjoy.

6)   You will get 6 servings in total.

Nutritional facts per serving:

Serving size: 150g

Calories: 230kcal

Carbohydrates: 27g

Protein: 5g

Fat: 11g

Fiber: 3g

==================

Baked Asparagus

What ingredients you will need:

1 teaspoon sea salt

1/2 teaspoon ground black pepper

1 tablespoon lemon juice (optional)

1 1/2 tablespoons grated Parmesan cheese (optional)

1 clove garlic, minced (optional)

1 bunch thin asparagus spears, trimmed

3 tablespoons olive oil

Directions:

1)   First of all preheat oven to 425 degrees F. In a mixing bowl mix all ingredients and make a mixture. Now coat this prepared mixture on asparagus.

2) Take a baking dish and place coated asparagus in this baking dish.

3)   Place baking dish in oven for baking process and bake it for 10 to 15 minutes.

4) Baked Asparagus is ready to serve. Serve and enjoy.

5) You will get 4 servings in total.

Nutritional facts per serving:

Serving size: 80g

Calories: 130kcal

Carbohydrates: 7g

Protein: 5g

Fat: 11g

Fiber: 3g

===================

Shrimp Scampi Bake

What ingredients you will need:

1 tablespoon chopped garlic

1 tablespoon chopped fresh parsley

2 pounds medium raw shrimp, shelled, deveined, with tails attached

1 cup butter

2 tablespoons prepared Dijon-style mustard

1 tablespoon fresh lemon juice

Directions:

1)   First of all preheat oven to 425 degrees F.

2)   Take a small size sauce pan and heat up all ingredients in it expect shrimp on medium heat.

3)   Wait that butter melts completely and turn off the stove.

4)   Take a baking dish and place shrimps in it and then pour butter mixture on top of shrimps in baking dish.

5)   Place this baking dish in preheated oven for baking process and bake it in oven for to 20 minutes.

6)   Serve and enjoy.

7)   This original recipe will give you servings in total.

Nutritional facts per serving:

Serving size: 240g

Calories: 430kcal

Carbohydrates: 2g

Protein: 35g

Fat: 29g

Fiber: 0g

= = = = = = = = = = = = = = = = = = = =

Honey Carrots And Parsnips

What ingredients you will need:

1/4 cup honey

salt and ground black pepper to taste

3 carrots, peeled

3 parsnips, peeled

2 tablespoons olive oil

Directions:

1)   First of all preheat oven to 350 degrees F.

2)   Take a baking dish and place carrots and parsnips in it. Now pour olive oil on top of it.

3)   Finally add honey and sprinkle salt and pepper on vegetables. Coat all ingredients very well on vegetables.

4)   Now put baking dish in oven for baking and bake it for 40 to 45 minutes. Make sure that vegetables are tender.

5)   Serve and enjoy. This original recipe will give you 4 servings in total.

Nutritional facts per serving:

Serving size: 140g

Calories: 220kcal

Carbohydrates: 42g

Protein: 2g

Fat: 7g

Fiber: 7g

= =

Mock Meatballs

What ingredients you will need:

1/2 teaspoon onion powder

1/4 teaspoon dried parsley

1/2 cup egg substitute

1 cup crushed saltine crackers

1/2 cup shredded Cheddar cheese

1/4 teaspoon garlic powder

1 cup chopped pecans

Directions:

1) First of all preheat oven to 350 degrees F.

2) Take a mixing bowl and add all ingredients in it. Now mix all ingredients very well and make a mixture.

3) Form egg size balls from prepared mixture.

4) Take a baking dish and make it greasy with the help of cooking spray. Now place prepared meatballs in baking dish.

5) Put baking dish in oven for baking. Bake it for 10 to 15 minutes.

6) Mock Meatballs are ready to serve.

7) You will get almost 12 meatballs from this recipe.

8) Serve and enjoy.

Nutritional facts per serving:

Serving size: 120g

Calories: 250kcal

Carbohydrates: 5g

Protein: 10g

Fat: 17g

Fiber: 2g

===================

Baked Pineapple

What ingredients you will need:

1 (20 ounce) can pineapple

5 slices fresh bread crumbs

1 cup white sugar

1/4 pound butter, softened

4 eggs, beaten

Directions:

1)   First of all preheat oven to 350 degrees F.

2)   Take a medium size mixing bowl and mix cream sugar and butter in it. Now add eggs in it and then finally add pineapple after draining from can.

3)   Mix bread crumbs in it and then pour all this mixture in a baking dish.

4)   Place this baking dish in oven for baking process and bake it for 60 minutes.

5)   This original recipe will give you 6 servings in total.

6)   Serve and enjoy.

Nutritional facts per serving:

Serving size: 210g

Calories: 360kcal

Carbohydrates: 50g

Protein: 7g

Fat: 17g

Fiber: 2g

= = = = = = = = = = = = = = = = = = = =

Easy Oven Brown Rice

What ingredients you will need:

2 tablespoons butter

3 cups boiling water

1 1/2 cups brown rice

1 teaspoon salt

Directions:

1)   First of all preheat oven to 400 degrees F.

2)   Take a coverable casserole dish and add rice, butter and salt in it. pour water on top of rice in casserole dish.

3)   Cover baking dish and then place it in oven for baking process. Bake it in preheated oven for 60 minutes or unless rice are completely cooked.

4)   Serve hot and enjoy.

5)   This original recipe will give you 3 servings in total.

Nutritional facts per serving:

Serving size: 140g

Calories: 200kcal

Carbohydrates: 36g

Protein: 4g

Fat: 5g

Fiber: 2g

= = = = = = = = = = = = = = = = = = = =

Crescent Dogs

What ingredients you will need:

1 (8 ounce) can refrigerated crescent dinner rolls

8 hot dogs

4 slices American cheese, each cut into 6 strips

Directions:

1)   First of all preheat oven to 375 degrees F.

2)   Make narrow 1/2 inch holes on sides of hot dogs and insert cheese strips in these holes.

3)   Fold hot dogs in dough and place in baking dish

4)   Now put baking dish in preheated oven for baking process.

5)   Bake it in oven for 15 minutes. The color of rolls should be brown after baking.

6)   Crescent Dogs are ready to serve.

7)   Serve and enjoy. This original recipe will give you 8 servings in total.

Nutritional facts per serving:

Serving size: 200g

Calories: 330kcal

Carbohydrates: 13g

Protein: 11g

Fat: 25g

Fiber: 0g

= = = = = = = = = = = = = = = = = = = =

Turkey Meatballs

What ingredients you will need:

2 tablespoons onion powder

2 tablespoons garlic powder

1/2 cup Italian bread crumbs

1/4 cup thinly sliced baby spinach

1 egg

1 pound ground turkey

Directions:

1)   First of all preheat oven to 375 degrees F.

2)   Take a mixing bowl and add all ingredients in it along with ground turkey. Now mix all ingredients very well and make a mixture.

3)   Make eggs size balls from prepared mixture by rolling mixture on your palms.

4)   Take baking sheet and make it greasy with the help of cooking spray. Now place prepared turkey balls on this baking dish.

5)   Place this baking in the oven for baking process and bake it for 20 minutes in the oven. Make sure after baking the color of meatballs should be brown.

6)   Delicious Turkey Meatballs are ready to serve. Serve and enjoy.

7)   This original recipe will give you 4 servings in total.

Nutritional facts per serving:

Serving size: 210g

Calories: 360kcal

Carbohydrates: 15g

Protein: 35g

Fat: 15g

Fiber: 2g

========================

========================

Dumpy Chicken Wings

What ingredients you will need:

1/2 cup white vinegar

3 tablespoons water

1 cup white sugar

3 pounds chicken wings

1 egg, lightly beaten

1 cup all-purpose flour for coating

1 cup butter

3 tablespoons soy sauce

1/2 teaspoon garlic powder, or to taste

1 teaspoon salt

Directions:

1)   First of all preheat oven to 350 degrees F.

2)   After cutting every wing into 2 pieces dip them into beaten eggs.

3)   After dipping in beaten eggs coat dipped wings with flour.

4)   Heat up butter in a skillet and then fry wings in it and make them brown.

5)   After browning wings place them on a baking dish.

6)   On other hand in a mixing bowl mix all remaining ingredients and make a saucy mixture. Pour this mixture on top of wings.

7)   Now bake these wings in preheated oven for 35 to 45 minutes.

8)   Dumpy Chicken Wings are ready to serve.

9)   Serve and enjoy.

10) This original recipe will give you 6 servings in total.

= = = = = = = = = = = = = = = = = = = =

Avocado Baked Eggs

What ingredients you will need:

1 pinch cayenne pepper

1/4 cup crumbled cooked bacon

1 tablespoon chopped fresh chives

1 avocado, halved and pitted

2 eggs

salt and ground black pepper to taste

Directions:

1)   First of all preheat oven to 350 degrees F.

2)   Take a ramekin dish and place pitted and halved avocado in it. Now pour egg in each piece of avocado. Sprinkle salt, pepper and cayenne pepper on top of it.

3)   Place this dish in the oven for baking process. Bake it in preheated oven for 15 minutes.

4)   Avocado Baked Eggs are ready to serve. Serve and enjoy.

5)   This original recipe will give you 1 serving in total.

Nutritional facts per serving:

Serving size: 220g

Calories: 350kcal

Carbohydrates: 10g

Protein: 17g

Fat: 29g

Fiber: 7g

= = = = = = = = = = = = = = = = = = =

Baked Salmon

What ingredients you will need:

1 tablespoon lemon juice

1 tablespoon fresh parsley, chopped

6 tablespoons light olive oil

2 cloves garlic, minced

1 teaspoon dried basil

1 teaspoon ground black pepper

1 teaspoon salt

2 (6 ounce) fillets salmon

Directions:

1) In a mixing bowl mix all ingredients except salmon and make a coating mixture. Now coat fillets of salmon with prepared mixture and place them in refrigerator for 1 hour. This will allow it to marinate.

2) Preheat oven to 375 degrees F. place salmon in a baking dish and bake them in preheated oven for 35 to 45 minutes.

3) Check tenderness of salmon with the help of fork.

4) Baked Salmon is ready to serve. Serve and enjoy.

5) This original recipe will give you 2 servings in total.

Nutritional facts per serving:

Serving size: 320g

Calories: 550kcal

Carbohydrates: 3g

Protein: 37g

Fat: 54g

Fiber: 0g

= = = = = = = = = = = = = = = = = = =

Garlic Roasted Broccoli with Parmesan Cheese

What ingredients you will need:

1/2 teaspoon coarse ground black pepper

1 head broccoli, washed and cut into bite-sized pieces

2 cloves garlic, minced

4 tablespoons extra virgin olive oil, divided

1 tablespoon lemon juice

1/2 teaspoon kosher salt

1/4 cup Dietz & Watson Shaved Parmesan Cheese

Directions:

1) First of all preheat oven to 425 degrees F.

2) After washing broccoli cut it into small pieces. Put broccoli in a baking dish after mixing with minced garlic.

3) Now pour olive oil on top of it and sprinkle salt and pepper.

4) Place baking dish in the oven for baking process and bake it for 20 to 25 minutes.

5) After baking add lemon juice and cheese on top of it.

6) Serve and enjoy. This original recipe will give you 6 servings in total.

Nutritional facts per serving:

Serving size: 80g

Calories: 120kcal

Carbohydrates: 4g

Protein: 4g

Fat: 14g

Fiber: 2g

=====================

River egg dinner

What ingredients you will need:

1/4 cup green onions, chopped

10 eggs

1/3 cup milk

1/2 teaspoon salt

4 dashes hot pepper sauce, or to taste

1/2 pound bacon - cooked, and chopped into bite-size pieces

1/3 cup mushrooms, sliced

1 (4 ounce) can black olives, drained

2 roma (plum) tomatoes, chopped

3/4 cup Colby-Monterey Jack cheese, shredded

Directions:

1)   First of all preheat oven to 350 degrees F.

2)   Take a mixing bowl and mix eggs and milk in it. Blend well both ingredients with the help of blender or electric mixer.

3)   Now add all remaining ingredients in it and make a mixture. Pour prepared mixture in a baking pan and then bake it in oven for 40 to 50 minutes.

4)   Make sure that eggs are firm in the center.

5)   Serve and enjoy. This original recipe will give you 6 servings in total.

Nutritional facts per serving:

Serving size: 220g

Calories: 390kcal

Carbohydrates: 5g

Protein: 20g

Fat: 21g

Fiber: 1g

= = = = = = = = = = = = = = = = = = = =

Dump Pepper Lime Chicken

What ingredients you will need:

1 teaspoon basil

1⁄4 teaspoon salt

4 chicken breasts

1⁄2 teaspoon lime peel

2 garlic cloves, minced

1⁄4 cup lime juice

1 teaspoon pepper

1 tablespoon olive oil

Directions:

1) Take a freezer bag and mix all ingredients in it. Seal this bag and put this into freezer for a night, this is good for marinating process.

2) Now before baking defrost it and pour all ingredients in a baking pan.

3) Put baking pan in oven and bake it at 350 degrees F for 30 minutes.

4) You can serve this dish with cooked rice.

5) Serve and enjoy.

6) This original recipe will give you 4 servings in total.

Nutritional facts per serving:

Serving size: 170g

Calories: 280kcal

Carbohydrates: 2g

Protein: 30g

Fat: 17g

Fiber: 1g

==================

Pineapple dump Chicken

What ingredients you will need:

1 cup pineapple preserves

2 teaspoons dry mustard

1 cup pineapple tidbits

1⁄2 lb chicken piece (breasts or thighs)

1⁄2 cup onion, chopped

1⁄4 cup butter, melted

1⁄2 cup ketchup

Directions:

1)   First of all preheat oven to 350 degrees F.

2)   Now take a mixing bowl and mix all ingredients in it except chicken. Coat chicken with prepared mixture.

3)   Place coated chicken in a greasy baking pan and pour all left over on top of chicken in the baking pan.

4)   Put baking pan in the oven for baking. Bake it in preheated oven for 35 minutes. Make sure chicken pieces are fully cooked.

5)   If you are using chicken pieces containing bones then increase time of baking to 45 to 60 minutes because they take more time in baking process.

6)   Serve and enjoy.

7)   This original recipe will give you 4 servings in total.

Nutritional facts per serving:

Serving size: 220g

Calories: 460kcal

Carbohydrates: 70g

Protein: 10g

Fat: 17g

Fiber: 2g

===================

Jeanettes Dump

What ingredients you will need:

1 (170 g) can crabmeat, drained

cracker, for serving

250 g cream cheese (lite is fine)

1 (250 ml) bottle tomato base seafood sauce

Directions:

1)   In this recipe we will use a serving platter. First of all add cream cheese on a serving platter.

2)   Put crabmeat on top of cream cheese and then finally pour seafood sauce on top of it.

3)   Serve prepared Jeanettes Dump with crakers.

4)   Serve and enjoy.

5)   This original recipe will give you 6 servings in total.

Nutritional facts per serving:

Serving size: 50g

Calories: 170kcal

Carbohydrates: 2g

Protein: 9g

Fat: 15g

Fiber: 0g

= =

Spiced Citrus Dump Chicken

What ingredients you will need:

1⁄2 teaspoon pepper

1⁄2 teaspoon seasoning salt

1 1⁄2 lbs chicken pieces (breasts, thighs, or wings)

2 tablespoons olive oil

2 tablespoons lime juice

2 tablespoons orange juice

2 tablespoons lemon juice

2 tablespoons chili powder

2 tablespoons paprika

1⁄4 teaspoon cayenne (or more)

Directions:

1)   First of all preheat oven to 350 degrees F.

2)   Take a freezer bag and mix all ingredients in it. Seal this bag and put this into freezer for a night, this is good for marinating process.

3)   Now before baking defrost it and pour all ingredients in a baking pan.

4)   Now this is time for baking it. Place this pan in oven for baking process and bake it for 35 minutes.

5)   If you are using chicken pieces containing bones then increase time of baking to 45 to 60 minutes because they take more time in baking process.

6)   After baking check it with fork that chicken in completely cooked or not.

7)   Serve and enjoy.

8)   This original recipe will give you 4 servings in total.

Serving size: 150g

Calories: 320kcal

Carbohydrates: 6g

Protein: 21g

Fat: 23g

Fiber: 3g

= = = = = = = = = = = = = = = = = = =

Honey Glazed dump Chicken

What ingredients you will need:

1/2 cup honey

1 1/2 lbs chicken pieces (breasts, thighs, or wings)

1/4 cup butter, Melted

1/8 cup soy sauce

Directions:

1)   First of all preheat oven to 350 degrees F.

2)   In a baking dish add chicken along with other ingredients and then coat chicken pieces with all other ingredients in the baking dish by turning chicken pieces for several times….

3)   Place this baking dish in preheated oven and bake it for 35 minutes.

4)   If you are using chicken pieces containing bones then increase time of baking to 45 to 60 minutes because they take more time in baking process.

5)   Serve and enjoy.

6)   This original recipe will give you 4 servings in total.

Nutritional facts per serving:

Serving size: 170g

Calories: 420kcal

Carbohydrates: 36g

Protein: 21g

Fat: 27g

Fiber: 1g

- -

Lemon Dill Chicken

What ingredients you will need:

1 teaspoon lemon zest

4 boneless skinless chicken breast halves

1 cup low-fat sour cream

1 tablespoon minced fresh dill

1 teaspoon lemon pepper seasoning

Directions:

1)   Take a casserole dish and make it greasy with the help of cooking spray.

2) Mix all ingredients except chicken pieces and make lemon dill sauce.

3)   Spread ¼ spoon of lemon dill sauce in casserole dish and then place chicken pieces on top of it.

4) Spread all remaining lemon dill sauce on top of chicken pieces.

5) Now bake it in oven at 425 degrees F for 30 to 35 minutes.

6)   Chicken should be tender after baking.

7)   Serve and enjoy.

8) This original recipe will give you 4 servings in total.

Nutritional facts per serving:

Serving size: 180g

Calories: 210kcal

Carbohydrates: 3g

Protein: 29g

Fat: 9g

Fiber: 1g

========================

Sticky Chicky Dump Chicken

What ingredients you will need:

3 tablespoons ketchup

1 1/2 lbs chicken pieces

2 tablespoons oil (optional)

1 tablespoon soy sauce

3 tablespoons smooth peanut butter

Directions:

1) First of preheat oven to 350 degrees F.

2) Now mix all ingredients except chicken and blend them well to make a mixture.

3) Coat chicken pieces with prepared mixture and place them in a baking sheet.

4) Bake it in preheated oven for 30 to 45 minutes.

5) If you are using chicken pieces containing bones then increase time of baking to 45 to 60 minutes because they take more time in baking process.

6) Serve and enjoy.

7) This original recipe will give you 4 servings in total.

Nutritional facts per serving:

Serving size: 100g

Calories: 310kcal

Carbohydrates: 6g

Protein: 21g

Fat: 22g

Fiber: 1g

= = = = = = = = = = = = = = = = = = = =

Dump Meatloaf

What ingredients you will need:

2 teaspoons garlic (minced)

3⁄4 cup colby-monterey jack cheese (shredded)

2 1⁄2 lbs ground beef

2 cups breadcrumbs (plain)

2 teaspoons sea salt (celtic)

1 (10 3/4 ounce) can cream of celery soup

4 large eggs

1⁄3 cup parsley (dried)

2 tablespoons basil (dried)

3⁄4 cup milk

1 tablespoon lemon pepper

Directions:

1)   First of preheat oven to 350 degrees F.

2) Take a mixing bowl and add all ingredients in it including ground meat. Now mix all these with the help of wooden spoon.

3)   After mixing it make a loaf of it and place it in a baking dish.

4)   Now place this baking dish in oven for baking process and bake it for 60 minutes in preheated oven.

5)   The color of meatloaf should be brown.

6)   Serve and enjoy.

7)   This original recipe will give you 12 servings in total.

Nutritional facts per serving:

Serving size: 180g

Calories: 350kcal

Carbohydrates: 15g

Protein: 25g

Fat: 21g

Fiber: 1g

= = = = = = = = = = = = = = = = = = = =

Dessert recipes

Peach Dump Cake

What ingredients you will need:

2 cups brown sugar

2 (16 ounce) bags frozen peaches

1 (18 ounce) box white cake mix

1 (21 ounce) can crushed pineapple

1/2 cup melted butter

Directions:

1)   Take a baking pan and dump pineapple pieces in the bottom of it. Do not forget to add drained pineapple in it.

2)   Now make second layer of peaches on top of pineapple in the baking pan. Sprinkle cake mix and sugar on top of it respectively.

3)   Finally pour melted butter on it and place this baking pan in oven for baking.

4)   Bake it in oven at 350 degrees F for 45 minutes.

5)   Serve and enjoy.

6)   This original recipe will give you 15 servings in total.

Nutritional facts per serving:

Serving size: 170g

Calories: 390kcal

Carbohydrates: 75g

Protein: 3g

Fat: 10g

Fiber: 2g

=====================

Cherry Dump Cake

What ingredients you will need:

1⁄2 cup margarine, melted

1⁄2 cup pecan pieces

21 ounces cherry pie filling

21 ounces apple pie filling

18 1⁄4 ounces yellow cake mix

Directions:

1)   Preheat oven to 350 degrees F.

2)   Take a 9X13 inch baking dish. Now pour apple and cherry pie filling in the bottom of this baking pan.

3)   Make a layer of cake mix on top of it and then add melted margarine on it. Finally add pecans and then it is ready for baking.

4)   Bake it in preheated oven for 1 hour.

5)   Serve and enjoy.

6)   This original recipe will give you 12 servings in total.

Nutritional facts per serving:

Serving size: 150g

Calories: 390kcal

Carbohydrates: 60g

Protein: 3g

Fat: 16g

Fiber: 2g

= = = = = = = = = = = = = = = = = = = =

Strawberry Dump Cake

What ingredients you will need:

1 cup margarine

1 cup nuts, chopped

1 (15 ounce) can crushed pineapple with juice

1 (15 ounce) can strawberry pie filling

1 box yellow cake mix

Directions:

1)   Preheat oven to 325 degrees F.

2)   Take a 13 x 9 x 2-inch greasy baking pan and dump pineapple in the bottom of it.

3)   Now add pie filling on top of pineapple layer and then sprinkle cake mix on it.

4)   Pour melted butter on it and then place this baking pan in oven for baking process.

5)   Bake it in oven 45 minutes.

6)   Serve and enjoy.

7)   This original recipe will give you 12 servings in total.

Nutritional facts per serving:

Serving size: 130g

Calories: 410kcal

Carbohydrates: 50g

Protein: 5g

Fat: 31g

Fiber: 2g

= = = = = = = = = = = = = = = = = = = =

Simple Apple Spice Dump Cake

What ingredients you will need:

1 tablespoon granulated sugar

3⁄4 cup butter

1 cup chopped nuts

1 (18 1/4 ounce) box spice cake mix

2 (21 ounce) cans apple pie filling

1 teaspoon ground cinnamon

1 teaspoon ground nutmeg

1 teaspoon ground allspice

Directions:

1)   Preheat oven to 325 degrees F.

2)   Take a 13 x 9-inch baking pan and add apple pie filling in the bottom of it.

3)   In a mixing bowl mix nutmeg, allspice, sugar and cinnamon and then sprinkle this mixture on pie filling layer.

4)   Make a layer of cake mix and then add butter and nuts.

5)   Bake it in preheated oven for 45 to 60 minutes. Make sure that after baking color of cake should be brown.

6)   Serve and enjoy.

7)   This original recipe will give you 12 servings in total.

Nutritional facts per serving:

Serving size: 170g

Calories: 450kcal

Carbohydrates: 60g

Protein: 4g

Fat: 24g

Fiber: 3g

====================

Pineapple Dump Cake

What ingredients you will need:

1⁄2 cup butter, melted

1 cup coconut

1 package yellow cake mix

1 (20 ounce) can pineapple, undrained

1 cup chopped nuts

Directions:

1)   Take a 13x9-inch size baking pan and make it little greasy with the help of cooking spray….

2)   Now make 2 layers of coconut and cake mix respectively.

3)   Add melted butter and then make final layer of nuts on top of it.

4)   Place baking pan in oven and bake it for 40 minutes at 350 degrees F.

5)   Serve and enjoy.

6)   This original recipe will give you 12 servings in total.

Nutritional facts per serving:

Serving size: 140g

Calories: 470kcal

Carbohydrates: 53g

Protein: 6g

Fat: 27g

Fiber: 4g

= =

Blueberry Dump Cake

What ingredients you will need:

1⁄2 cup butter

1 package yellow lemon cake mix

1 1⁄2 cups pineapple, crushed

2 cups blueberries (frozen or fresh)

1⁄2-1 cup walnut pieces

Directions:

1)   Take a 13x9-inch size baking pan and make it little greasy with the help of cooking spray….

2)   Now dump pineapple and berries pie filling in the bottom of baking pan.

3)   Sprinkle cake mix on top of pie fillings ad then pour melted butter on top of it.

4)   Finally sprinkle nuts and place this baking pan in oven for baking process.

5)   Bake it in oven at 375 Degrees F for 30 to 50 minutes.

6)   Serve and enjoy.

7)   This original recipe will give you 12 servings in total.

Nutritional facts per serving:

Serving size: 80g

Calories: 270kcal

Carbohydrates: 40g

Protein: 6g

Fat: 16g

Fiber: 3g

==================

Pumpkin Pie Dump Cake

What ingredients you will need:

2 tablespoons cinnamon

1/2 teaspoon ginger

1/2 teaspoon nutmeg

1 (18 1/2 ounce) box yellow cake mix

1 (29 ounce) can pumpkin puree, without spices

3 eggs

1 (13 ounce) can evaporated milk

1 cup butter, Melted

1 1/2 cups sugar

Directions:

1)   In this recipe we will use 9x13 inch ungreased baking pan.

2)   Preheat oven to 350 degrees F.

3)   In a mixing bowl mix all ingredients except cake mix and butter and make a mixture.

4)   Now add this mixture in baking pan and then add cake mix on top of it.

5)   Pour melted butter on layer of cake mix and then place this baking pan in preheated oven for baking.

6)   Bake it in oven for 45 to 60 minutes.

7)   Allow it to cool down before serving.

8)   Serve and enjoy. You will get 10 servings in total.

Nutritional facts per serving:

Serving size: 240g

Calories: 700kcal

Carbohydrates: 100g

Protein: 10g

Fat: 36g

Fiber: 3g

====================

Tropical Dump Cake

What ingredients you will need:

1⁄2 cup butter or 1⁄2 cup margarine, melted

1 cup flaked coconut

1 cup chopped pecans (optional)

1 (21 ounce) can cherry pie filling

1 (20 ounce) can crushed pineapple with juice

1 (18 ounce) box yellow cake mix

1⁄2 cup butter or 1⁄2 cup margarine, cut into pieces

Directions:

1) In this recipe we will use 9x13 inch greasy baking pan.

2) First of all pour cherry pie filling and pineapple in the baking pan.

3) Now sprinkle cake mix on top of it.

4) Finally pour butter on cake mix and then sprinkle nuts and flaked coconut on top of it.

5) Now bake it in oven at 350 degrees F for 60 minutes.

6) Serve and enjoy. This original recipe will give you 10 servings in total.

Nutritional facts per serving:

Serving size: 200g

Calories: 520kcal

Carbohydrates: 32g

Protein: 13g

Fat: 26g

Fiber: 2g

==================

Black Forest Dump Cake

What ingredients you will need:

1 cup chopped pecans

1⁄2 cup butter or 1⁄2 cup margarine, melted

1 (8 ounce) can crushed pineapple

1 (21 ounce) can cherry pie filling

1 package devil's food cake mix

Directions:

1) Take a 13x9x2 inch greased baking pan and place pineapple in the bottom of it.

2) Now pour pie filling on top of pineapple pieces.

3) Sprinkle cake mix on top of it and then pecan nuts.

4) Pour melted butter on pecan nuts and then place this baking pan in oven for baking process.

5) Bake it in oven at 350 degrees F for 35 to 40 minutes.

6) Allow it to cool down and then it is ready to serve.

7) Serve and enjoy. This original recipe will give you 10 servings in total.

Nutritional facts per serving:

Serving size: 160g

Calories: 460kcal

Carbohydrates: 60g

Protein: 5g

Fat: 25g

Fiber: 2.3g

====================

Chocolate Cherry dump Cake

What ingredients you will need:

2 1⁄4 ounces of chopped pecans

1⁄8 cup white sugar

2 (21 ounce) cans cherry pie filling

1 (16 ounce) box chocolate cake mix

1 cup butter, sliced into 12 pieces each

Directions:

1)   Take a baking pan and dump pie filling in it.

2)   Sprinkle cake mix on top of pie filling,s layer. Now sprinkle pecan nuts on it.

3)   Pour melted butter on top of cake mix and then finally make a final layer of sugar.

4)   Now bake it in oven for 30 to 45 minutes at 350 degrees F.

5)   Allow it to cool down and then it is ready to serve.

6)   Serve and enjoy. This original recipe will give you 12 servings in total.

Nutritional facts per serving:

Serving size: 160g

Calories: 450kcal

Carbohydrates: 60g

Protein: 3g

Fat: 25g

Fiber: 2g

Banana Split Dump Cake

What ingredients you will need:

1⁄2 cup margarine, cut in pieces

1 cup coconut

1⁄2 cup crushed nuts

1 (21 ounce) can strawberry pie filling

1 (20 ounce) can crushed pineapple (don't drain)

1 white cake mix, dry

For topping

sliced banana

whipped cream

chocolate syrup

Directions:

1)   Take a 9x13 inch baking pan and make it greasy with the help of cooking spray.

2) First of all dump pie filling in the bottom of baking pan and then place pineapple on top of this layer.

3)   Sprinkle cake mix and then pour margarine on it.

4) Finally make last layer of coconut and nuts and then bake it in oven for 60 to 75 minutes at 325 degrees F.

5) Allow it to cool down and then top it with toping ingredients.

6)   Serve and enjoy. This original recipe will give you 24 servings in total.

Nutritional facts per serving:

Serving size: 60g

Calories: 180kcal

Carbohydrates: 22g

Protein: 2g

Fat: 10g

Fiber: 2g

= = = = = = = = = = = = = = = = = = =